GRANDPARENTS
ARE
GREAT

(the book every grandparent wants)

CHARLES L. ALLEN

A BARBOUR BOOK

Scripture quoted by permission. Quotations designated (NIV) are from THE HOLY BIBLE: NEW INTERNATIONAL VERSION. Copyright 1973, 1978, 1984 by The International Bible Society.

Published by Barbour and Company, Inc.,
        P.O. Box 719
        Uhrichsville, Ohio 44683

Typesetting by Typetronix, Inc., Cape Coral, Florida

ISBN   1-55748-313-2

Printed in the United States of America

1 2 3 4 5 / 97 96 95 94 93 92

ACKNOWLEDGMENTS

The quotation from *Liguorian* is excerpted from Lucid Intervals and appeared in July 1968 issue.

The quotation by Earl Hanson first appeared in *Education*, February 3, 1969, issue.

The quotation by Chet Huntley was excerpted from *The Generous Years; Remembrances of a Frontier Boyhood* by Chet Huntley, published by Random House, Inc., copyright 1968.

The quotation by Cecil B. Murphey used by permission of author.

Quotation from Herbert V. Prochnow and Herbert V. Prochnow, Jr. used by permission of Herbert V. Prochnow.

Malcolm Forbes quotation: Reprinted by permission of FORBES magazine, January 15, 1970. © Forbes Inc., 1970.

The selection from *Grit* is from the May 10, 1970, issue.

E. Paul Hovey excerpt: From the book THE TREASURY OF INSPIRATIONAL ANECDOTES, QUOTATIONS AND ILLUSTRATIONS by E. Paul Hovey, copyright © 1959 by Fleming H. Revell. Used by permission of Baker Book House.

Elton Trueblood excerpt: From *The Life We Prize* by Elton Trueblood, copyright © 1951 by Harper and Brothers. Reprinted by permission of HarperCollins Publishers

I

Nothing makes a child smarter than being a grandchild.

GRANDPARENTS ARE GREAT

Here is a way to punish children—keep them away from their grandparents.

As the bus was filling up, a man got on and was about to sit down next to a woman when he asked if she were a grandmother.

"Yes," she answered proudly, "twice."

With that, the man moved to another seat where he asked the same question, then he moved again.

Upon receiving a negative answer from the third person, he sat down with a sigh of relief.

"I'm glad you are not a grandparent, so I will tell you about my grandchildren."

ANONYMOUS

GRANDPARENTS ARE GREAT

The importance of grandparents in the life of little children is immeasurable. A young child with the good fortune to have grandparents nearby benefits in countless ways. It has a place to share its joys, its sorrows, to find a sympathetic and patient listener, to be loved.

A child without grandparents can feel the lack of roots and a lack of connectiveness. It misses a chance to link up with the past . . . questions and answers about the "old days" locate a child historically in his own small world. It provides a sense of inner security and a feeling of belonging.

EDWARD WAKIN

Grandparent: Something so simple a child can operate it.

A gentleman passed his granddaughter's room one night and overheard her repeating the alphabet in an oddly reverent way. "What on earth are you up to?" he asked.

"I'm saying my prayers," explained the little girl. "But I can't think of exactly the right words tonight, so I'm just saying all the letters. God will put them together for me, because he knows what I am thinking."

SOURCE UNKNOWN

GRANDPARENTS ARE GREAT

A portly gentleman was in the toy department and was obviously taken with a toy train that whistled, belched smoke, deposited milk cans, and, in fact, did virtually everything a real freight train does.

"I'll take it, " he said finally.

"Good," approved the clerk. "I am sure your grandson will love playing with it."

"You are absolutely right," agreed the gentleman thoughtfully. "I'd better have two."

SOURCE UNKNOWN

GRANDPARENTS ARE GREAT

One good thing you can say for children is that they never pull out pictures of their grandparents.

LIGUORIAN

Why is it that the boy you were sure wasn't good enough for your daughter turned out to be the father of the world's smartest grandchildren?

SOURCE UNKNOWN

Sitting one afternoon with three noisy preschoolers, the grandmother was trying to quiet them by reading nursery rhymes. When she came to "the cow jumped over the moon," little Johnny asked, "Grandmother, did the cow blast off from Cape Canaveral?"

SOURCE UNKNOWN

GRANDPARENTS ARE GREAT

A woman was asked if she had yet made a long trip to California to visit her son and his new wife.

"No," she replied, "I've been waiting until they have their new baby."

"Oh, I see," said the friend," you do not want to spend money on a trip until then."

"No, it isn't that," the woman explained. "You see, I have a theory that grandmothers are more welcome than mothers-in-law."

EARL WILSON

A certain grandmother was so delighted that her grandchildren were coming for a visit that she gave five dollars to the church. The following Sunday, after the children left, she gave ten dollars!

Our greatest obligation to our children and grandchildren is to prepare them to understand and to deal effectively with the world in which they will live—not with the world we have known or the world we would prefer to have.

GRAYSON KIRK

GRANDPARENTS ARE GREAT

My teenage granddaughter wrote me plaintively that her five-year-old brother would not mind her.

I replied, "It is aggravating that Mark misbehaves, but he is a fine boy. You know, Susan, there are four ways to persuade people to do what you want:

"One, pay them.

"Two, make them because you are stronger.

"Three, entertain them, play games—they laugh with you and they 'go along' because you're a playmate.

"Four, love them, show it, and they love you back. They want to do what pleases you.

"To raise children takes all four, but the best results come from a whole lot of number four."

EARL H. HANSON

GRANDPARENTS ARE GREAT

You can do anything with children if you only play with them.

JOHANN VON GOETHE

The old folks wonder *what* the younger generation is coming to—while the young people wonder *when* the older generation is coming to.

BEN BERGER

A Sunday school teacher suddenly stopped reading a passage in the Bible and asked the youngsters, "Why do you believe in God?"

She got a variety of answers, some full of simple faith, others obviously insincere. The one that stunned her came from a young boy. He answered, "I guess it just runs in the family."

SOURCE UNKNOWN

I have been unable to sort out the overlapping attitudes of respect and affection I had for the four adults who made up so much of my childhood...

I learned that Grandma and Mother were unsatisfactory sources of information about animal habits and ranch life. Frequently, I was informed that small boys had no need of answers to such questions. Dad too was something less than candid. But Grandpa told me what I wanted to know . . . bluntly and somewhat vividly. What I failed to learn from him, I picked up easily from the hired hands who worked on the ranch later. Somehow, every association with Grandpa held the promise or the possibility of high adventure.

He never realized, I suppose, what he did for the ego of a small boy when he waived aside the misgivings of Grandma and Mother and took me into town with him. Those were the moments of triumph!

Chet Huntley

GRANDPARENTS ARE GREAT

What gift has God bestowed on man that is so dear to him as his own children?

CHARLES DICKENS

But from everlasting to everlasting the Lord's love is with those who fear him, and his righteousness with their children's children.

PSALM 103:17 (NIV)

GRANDPARENTS ARE GREAT

Don't stop growing as an individual. Being a grandparent is a new stage of life—not the final one.

CECIL B. MURPHEY

II

To me, old age is always fifteen years older than I am.

BERNARD BARUCH

GRANDPARENTS ARE GREAT

I know of no fallacy greater, or more widely believed, than the statement that youth is the happiest time of life. As we advance in years we really grow happier, if we live intelligently. The universe is spectacular, and it is a free show. Increase of difficulties and responsibilities strengthens and enriches the mind and adds to the variety of life.

To live abundantly is like climbing a mountain or a tower. To say that youth is happier than maturity is like saying that the view from the bottom of the tower is better than the view from the top. As we ascend, the range of our view widens immensely; the horizon is pushed farther away. Finally, as we reach the summit it is as if we had the world at our feet.

WILLIAM LYON PHELPS

GRANDPARENTS ARE GREAT

Forty is the old age of youth;
Fifty is the youth of old age.

VICTOR HUGO

The Seven Ages of People:

1. At twenty work was play, and we kept busy all the day.

2. At thirty we had found our stride, and sailed serenely with the tide.

3. At forty we enjoyed each day and filled the hours a fruitful way.

GRANDPARENTS ARE GREAT

4. At fifty life was good to her and him, and we looked very fit and trim.

5. At sixty we pressed on with zest, and still resolved to do our best.

6. At seventy we were going strong, and carried in our hearts a song.

7. At eighty we spoke like a sage, and boasted loudly of our age!

ANONYMOUS

GRANDPARENTS ARE GREAT

No one grows old by living—only by losing interest in living.

MARIE BENTON RAY

Age is opportunity no less
Than youth itself, though in another dress
and as the evening twilight fades away
The sky is filled with stars, invisible by day.

HENRY WADSWORTH LONGFELLOW

GRANDPARENTS ARE GREAT

While we've youth in our hearts, we can never grow old.

OLIVER WENDELL HOLMES

You know you are getting old when the candles cost more than the cake.

BOB HOPE

A wise man who had lived buoyantly through fourscore years was asked, "Which is the happiest season of life?"

He replied thoughtfully, "When spring comes, and in the soft air the buds are breaking on the trees, and they are covered with blossoms, I think, how beautiful is spring!

"And when summer comes, and covers the trees and bushes with heavy foliage; and singing birds mingle with the branches, I think, how beautiful is summer!

GRANDPARENTS ARE GREAT

"When autumn loads them with golden fruit, and their leaves bear the gorgeous tint of frost, I think, how beautiful is autumn!

"And when it is sore winter, and there is neither foliage nor fruit, then when I look up through the leafless branches and see, as I can see in no other season, the shining stars of heaven, I think, how beautiful is the Winter of life!"

HERBERT V. PROCHNOW, JR.

GRANDPARENTS ARE GREAT

Few people know how to be old.

FRANCOIS, DUC DE LA ROCHEFOUCAULD

It is magnificent to grow old, if one keeps young.

HARRY EMERSON FOSDICK

GRANDPARENTS ARE GREAT

Age is a quality of mind.
If you've left your dreams behind,
If hope is cold;
If you no longer look ahead,
If your ambition fires are dead,
Then you are old.

EDWARD ZUCK

GRANDPARENTS ARE GREAT

Six-year-old grandson: "Granddad, were you in the Ark with Noah?"

Granddad: "Why no, I wasn't, honey."

Grandson: "Then why weren't you drowned?"

> If wrinkles must be written upon our brows,
> let them not be written upon the heart.
> The spirit should never grow old.
>
> JAMES A. GARFIELD

GRANDPARENTS ARE GREAT

Senior citizen, after listening to an old song, said: "There's music to my years."

A. S. FLAUMENHAFT

Grant me, sound of body and of mind, to pass an old age lacking neither honor nor the lyre.

HORACE

If growing old saddens you, then why cry for those who cease to?

MALCOLM FORBES

GRANDPARENTS ARE GREAT

I wouldn't swap one wrinkle of my face for all the elixirs of youth. All the wrinkles represent a smile, a grimace of pain and disappointment . . . some part of being fully alive.

HELEN HAYES

Blisters are a painful experience, but if you get enough blisters in the same place, they will eventually produce a callus. That is what we call maturity.

HERBERT MILLER

GRANDPARENTS ARE GREAT

Strong meat belongeth to them that are of full age.

HEBREWS 5:14 (KJV)

All experience is an arch wherethrough
Gleams that untravelled world whose margin fades
For ever and for ever when I move.

ALFRED, LORD TENNYSON

GRANDPARENTS ARE GREAT

In the central place of every heart, there is a recording chamber; so long as it receives messages of beauty, hope, cheer, and courage, so long as you are young.

When the wires are all down and your heart is covered with the snows of pessimism and the ices of cynicism, then, and only then, are you grown old.

GENERAL DOUGLAS MACARTHUR

It was at a state fair. The spectacular act was a dive from 100 feet up into a shallow tank of water. Out came the diver, a man about 80 years old.

He addressed the crowd. "Do you think it is right for a man my age to make this dangerous dive?"

The stunned audience yelled in sympathy, "No, don't dive! Don't do it! Don't do it!"

"Thank you, kind people," replied the man. "The next show will be at 7:30 tonight."

HENRY E. LEARD

Most old people are senile, lonely, and too sick to carry on normal activities.

Those are among the leading myths about senior citizens, says Morton Teicher, director of the Center on Aging at the University of Miami. He explodes these falsehoods:

"Most old people are senile." The truth is that only about 2 to 3% of people over 65 are in mental hospitals. Less than 10% are disoriented or demented.

"Most old people feel miserable most of the time." The truth is that a majority of old people are just as happy as in their youth.

"A large proportion of old people live in nursing homes, mental hospitals, and homes for the aged." The truth is that less than 5% of senior citizens are in institutions.

"When old people drive, they have more accidents." The truth is that drivers over the age of 65 have a much lower accident rate than drivers under 30.

"Most old people are lonely." The truth is that most old people are not isolated. A majority belong to churches, synagogues and other voluntary organizations. They have friends and relatives within easy visiting distance.

LEONARD SANDLER

GRANDPARENTS ARE GREAT

To be seventy years young is sometimes far more cheerful and hopeful than to be forty years old.

OLIVER WENDELL HOLMES

Some people say they don't want to live to be 100—but they're not 99.

SOURCE UNKNOWN

GRANDPARENTS ARE GREAT

How old are you? Youth is not a time of life—it is a state of mind!

You are as young as: your faith, your hope, your confidence.

You are as old as: your doubt, your despair, your fear.

H.B. VAN VELZER

GRANDPARENTS ARE GREAT

We like the one about the grandparent who asked the grandchild how many states there are that you can name. The child named all fifty.

"That is wonderful," gushed the grandparent, "I certainly could not have done that at your age."

"Yes, and there were only thirteen of them then," commented the youngster.

SOURCE UNKNOWN

Chronological age is not your true age. Every person is different, and no two people born on the same day are really as old as each other by the time they get past middle age. Experts on aging around the world are working hard now on a whole new calendar of human life, based not on months or days or years but on analysis of the factors which contribute to homeostasis.

ROBERT RODALE

GRANDPARENTS ARE GREAT

A wise woman of 80 tells her friends as they reach 60:

"You have spent 60 years in preparation for life; you will now begin to live. At 60 you have learned what is worthwhile. You have conquered the worst forms of foolishness, you have reached a balanced period of life, knowing good from evil; what is previous, what is worthless.

"Danger is past, the mind is peaceful, evil is forgotten, the affections are strong, envy is weak. It is the happy age."

GRIT

GRANDPARENTS ARE GREAT

One day the Hodja (Turkish for "teacher") and his friends were discussing the merits of youth and old age. They all, except the Hodja, agreed that one's strength decreases as the years go by.

"I disagree," said the Hodja. "In my old age, I have the same strength that I had in my youth!"

"Explain!" his friends cried.

"Well, in the courtyard," explained the Hodja, "there is a massive stone. In my youth, I used to try to lift it. I never succeeded. Neither can I lift it now."

HELEN H. GREEN

GRANDPARENTS ARE GREAT

So long as enthusiasm lasts, so long is youth still with us.

DAVID STARR JORDAN

Wouldn't it be terrible if we were born old, and had to look forward to growing young, green, and silly?

Winter is on my head, but spring is in my heart.

VICTOR HUGO

GRANDPARENTS ARE GREAT

For grandparents, now is the time to live. All that has gone before has been largely preparation—one has discharged his or her obligations, made his or her contribution to society, founded a home, raised a family, and now the ultimate goal, life itself, is at hand.

HOWARD WHITMAN

GRANDPARENTS ARE GREAT

Never resent the years you have lived. Some people never had the opportunity of your years.

E. B. PRESCOTT

One pleasure of retirement is that you never have to be in a hurry. However, one of retirement's regrets is wondering why you ever were.

SOURCE UNKNOWN

GRANDPARENTS ARE GREAT

At sixty, one has passed most of the reefs and whirlpools. Excepting death, one has no enemies to meet .... That person has awakened to a new youth .... Ergo, that person is young.

GEORGE LUKS

No period of life, no position or circumstances, has a monopoly on success. Any age is the right age to start doing!

GERARD

Growing old is only a state of mind . . . brought on by gray hairs, false teeth, wrinkles, a big belly, short breath, constantly and totally pooped.

SOURCE UNKNOWN

III

God is glorified, not only by our groans,
but by our thanksgivings.

EDWIN PERCY WHIPPLE

Matthew Henry, the famous scholar, was once accosted by thieves and robbed of his purse. He wrote these words in his diary:

"Let me be thankful, first because I was never robbed before; second, because although they took my purse, they did not take my life; third, because although they took my all, it was not much. Fourth, because it was I who was robbed, not I who robbed."

SOURCE UNKNOWN

The worst moment for the atheist is when he is really thankful and has nobody to thank.

DANTE GABRIEL ROSSETTI

Praise changes things. Praise changes you. Try it! A song of praise in the prison of gloom or depression can open its doors:

"And at midnight Paul and Silas prayed, and sang praises unto God . . . . and immediately all the doors were opened, and every one's bands were loosed."

ACTS 16:25, 26 (KJV)

If anyone would tell you the shortest, surest way to happiness and all perfection, he must tell you to make it a rule to yourself to thank and praise God for everything that happens to you. For it is certain that whatever seeming calamity happens to you, if you thank and praise God for it, you turn it into a blessing.

WILLIAM LOW

Know therefore that the LORD your God is God; he is the faithful God, keeping his covenant of love to a thousand generations of those who love him and keep his commands.

DEUTERONOMY 7:9 (NIV)

"I have swept away your offenses like a cloud, your sins like the morning mist. Return to me, for I have redeemed you."

ISAIAH 44:22 (NIV)

GRANDPARENTS ARE GREAT

My heart leaps up when I behold
A rainbow in the sky;
So was it when my life began;
So it is now I am a man;
So be it when I shall grow old,
    Or let me die!

The Child is father of the Man;
And I could wish my days to be
Bound each to each by natural
    piety.

WILLIAM WORDSWORTH

IV

Better is a dry morsel, and quietness therewith,
than a house full of sacrifice with strife.

PROVERBS 17:1 (KJV)

A friend was saying, "When you find it difficult to remember names, you need to conjure up a picture in your mind. For example, if you want to remember the name of the poet Robert Burns, think of a policeman in London in flames. You see, 'Bobbie Burns.'"

"I see," the other person said. "But how am I to be sure it does not mean 'Robert Browning?'"

ANONYMOUS

A naive person is anyone who thinks you are interested when you ask how he or she is.

When I meet a man whose name I cannot remember, I give myself two minutes, then I always say, "And how is the old complaint?"

BENJAMIN DISRAELI

The older he grew, the less he spoke, and the more he said.

ANONYMOUS

GRANDPARENTS ARE GREAT

Love ever gives—
Forgives—outlives—
And even stands
With open hands.

And while it lives,
It gives,
For this is Love's prerogative—
To give—and give—and give.

JOHN OXEHAM

GRANDPARENTS ARE GREAT

It is a greater compliment to be trusted than to be loved.

GEORGE MacDONALD

Those who love deeply never grow old; they may die of old age, but they die young.

ARTHUR WING PINERO

GRANDPARENTS ARE GREAT

If you want to be loved, avoid criticism of those you want to love you .

Little said, sooner mended.

"But love your enemies, do good to them, and lend to them without expecting to get anything back. Then your reward will be great, and you will be sons of the Most High, because he is kind to the ungrateful and wicked. Be merciful, just as your Father is merciful.

"Do not judge, and you will not be judged. Do not condemn, and you will not be condemned. Forgive, and you will be forgiven."

Luke 6: 35-37 (NIV)

V

I do not read advertisements. I would spend all my time wanting things.
ARCHBISHOP OF CANTERBURY

It is almost as difficult to live within your income today as it was to live without one back in the '30s.

Money doesn't bring happiness. The one with ten million dollars isn't much happier than the one with nine million.

GRANDPARENTS ARE GREAT

Few of us can stand prosperity. Another man's, I mean.

MARK TWAIN

Big mouthfuls often choke.

ITALIAN PROVERB

Where your treasure is, there will your heart be also.

MATTHEW 6:21 (KJV)

After Oliver Wendell Holmes retired at past 90 years of age, his income was reduced. He remarked, "I have always been a prudent man, so this cut in pay will not hurt me; but I am distressed that I cannot continue to lay aside as much as usual for old age!"

SOURCE UNKNOWN

VI

Some people keep you from being lonely
when you wish you were.

GRANDPARENTS ARE GREAT

The world today does not understand, in either man or woman, the need to be alone. How inexplicable it seems. Anything else will be accepted as a better excuse. If one sets time aside for a . . . shopping expedition, that time is accepted as inviolable. But if one says: I cannot come because that is my hour to be alone, one is considered rude, egotistical or strange.

ANNE MORROW LINDBERGH

What is loneliness for you? You may be one of the lonely aged, the lonely poor, or the lonely youth. Loneliness is often experienced in a crowd.

Loneliness is different from aloneness. Loneliness is different from solitude. Loneliness is the feeling of being cut off from others, of being different from others.

WADE P. HUIE

Then you will call, and the LORD will answer; you will cry for help, and he will say: Here am I.

ISAIAH 58:9 (NIV)

"I will be a Father to you, and you will be my sons and daughters, says the Lord Almighty."

2 CORINTHIANS 6:18 (NIV)

GRANDPARENTS ARE GREAT

When we feel lonely it is good to remember how Admiral Byrd lived by himself for five months in a small shack in the Antarctic Zone. Blizzards blew all around his hut, and the temperature was sometimes as cold as eight-two degrees below zero.

Then he was terrified by a sudden discovery: Carbon dioxide was escaping from his stove. Try as hard as he could, Byrd was unable to fix it; when he attempted to make a repair, he would be almost overcome by the fumes. He could not turn off the stove for fear he would freeze. The nearest help, which was 123 miles away, could not reach him for months. He lost his ability to eat or sleep, and he was so weak he stayed in bed.

Admiral Byrd was forced to seek a power that was higher than his own. He reached out with his prayers and experienced the living touch of the presence of God. In his diary he wrote, "I am not alone!"

Admiral Byrd knew that One who loved him deeply was with him all the time, bringing him an experience of peace which would lead him to face the future with true spiritual strength.

E. PAUL HOVEY

VII

... I have learned, in whatsoever state I am, therewith to be content.

PHILIPPIANS 4:11 (KJV)

GRANDPARENTS ARE GREAT

I've shut my door on yesterday—
Its sorrows and mistakes;
I've looked within its gloomy walls
Past failures and heartaches.

And now I throw the key away!
To seek another room,
And furnish it with life and smiles
And every springtime bloom.

I've shut the door on yesterday
And thrown the key away—
Tomorrow holds no fears for me,
Since I have found today.

VIVIEN YEISER LARAMORE

GRANDPARENTS ARE GREAT

Turn backward, turn backward,
O time, in thy run,
For now I can see
How it should have been done.

ELINOR T. ROSE

Every person's life lies within the present; for the past is spent and done with, and the future is uncertain.

MARCUS ANTONIUS

GRANDPARENTS ARE GREAT

Grave of Winifred
Holthy

(1898-1935)

God give me work
Till my life shall end
And life
Till my work is done.

GRANDPARENTS ARE GREAT

One of the most tragic things about human nature is that all of us tend to put off living. We are all dreaming of some rose garden over the horizon instead of enjoying the roses that are blooming in our own backyard.

SOURCE UNKNOWN

Count your obligations,
Name them one by one,
And it will surprise you
What the Lord wants done!

GRANDPARENTS ARE GREAT

Love is always young and fair,
What to us is silver hair,
Faded cheeks or steps grown slow,
To the heart that beats below?
Since I kissed you mine alone,
You have never older grown.

EBEN E. REXFORD

GRANDPARENTS ARE GREAT

There are two days of the week upon which and about which I never worry. Two care-free days kept sacredly free from fear and apprehension. One of these days is yesterday; with all its pains and aches, all its faults and blunders, it has passed forever beyond the reach of my recall. Save for the beautiful memories, sweet and tender, that linger like the perfume of roses in the heart of the day that has gone, I have nothing to do with yesterday. It was mine; it is God's.

And the other day I do not worry about is tomorrow, with all its possibilities, adversities, its burdens, its perils, its large promise. Its sun will rise in roseate splendor, or behind a mask of clouds. But it will rise. Tomorrow—it will be mine.

There is left for myself, then, but one day of the week—today. Any man can fight the battles of today. Any woman can carry the burdens of just one day.

Therefore, I think, and I do, and I journey for but one day at a time. And while faithfully and dutifully I run my course, and work my appointed task on this one day, God the Almighty takes care of yesterday and tomorrow.

ROBERT J. BURDETTE

VIII

Nothing recedes like success.

GRANDPARENTS ARE GREAT

I'm against mandatory retirement. It ought to be left to individuals. It is a shame to assume that all fools are old fools. I've found there are more young fools than old fools. Nature has a way of getting rid of old fools.

SAM ERVIN

Complete idleness after a lifetime of work has been the undoing of many a person; just lying around in the sun renders many of us useless and only hastens demise. This is a cold fact being discovered by scores and scores of people whose retirement program called for complete idleness. It just did not work out for any of them.

ERNEST W. FAIN

Grandparents are Great

With maturity we find our independence. We stay away from the clubs that bore us. We wear our hair as we like. We go to bed when we feel like it. We don't have to ask anyone when we want the car. And we are more concerned with how our shoes fit than our sweaters.

ROBERT PETERSON

GRANDPARENTS ARE GREAT

Retirement can be:

a time to do some well-deserved relaxing;

an opportunity to see emotional tranquillity and engage in constructive leisure;

a release from the burdens of responsibility before they become too hard to deal with;

a chance to reintegrate one's life and even to embark on a second career.

SOURCE UNKNOWN

Think what the world would have missed had a retirement age been universally enforced in the past.

William Gladstone was prime minister of Great Britain at 83; Benjamin Franklin helped frame the Constitution of the United States at 80; Oliver Wendell Holmes retired from the United States Supreme Court at 91; Henry Ford, when past 80, again took up the presidency of the Ford Motor Company; and Alonzo Stagg was named "Football Man of the Year" at 81.

IX

Let us drink to our futures,

which, thank God,

are perfect!

GRANDPARENTS ARE GREAT

You can't do much about your ancestors, but you can influence your descendants enormously.

Toil, feel, think, hope; you will be sure to dream enough before you die, without arranging for it.

J. STERLING

GRANDPARENTS ARE GREAT

A reporter was interviewing a man who was believed to be the oldest resident in town. "May I ask how old you are?" the newsman inquired.

"I just turned a hundred this week," the man replied.

"Great! Do you suppose you'll see another hundred?" the reporter asked.

"Well," said the man thoughtfully, "I'm stronger now than when I started the first one hundred."

HERBERT V. PROCHNOW
HERBERT V. PROCHNOW, JR.

GRANDPARENTS ARE GREAT

I like the dreams of the future better than the history of the past.

THOMAS JEFFERSON

You are young at any age, if you are planning for tomorrow.

GRANDPARENTS ARE GREAT

When as a child
I laughed and wept—
Time crept!

When as a youth
I dreamed and talked—
Time walked!

When I became
A full-grown man—
Time ran!

GRANDPARENTS ARE GREAT

When as with the years
I older grew—
Time flew!

Soon I shall find
As I travel on—
Time gone!

ANONYMOUS

GRANDPARENTS ARE GREAT

Life is like riding a bicycle. You don't fall off until you stop pedaling.

CLAUDE PEPPER

In three words I can sum up everything I have learned about life: It goes on.

ROBERT FROST

GRANDPARENTS ARE GREAT

We have made at least a start on discovering the meaning of human life when we plant shade trees under which we know full well we will never sit.

ELTON TRUEBLOOD

Greatness of name in the father oft-times overwhelms the son; they stand too near one another. The shadow kills the growth: so much that we see the grandchild come more and oftener to be heir of the first.

BEN JONSON

GRANDPARENTS ARE GREAT

The query comes: How long is Life?
Threescore and ten the Good Book reads,
Is time enough for men to write
The record of his life in deeds?

Threescore and ten—how fast they fly!
Threescore and ten—they're almost gone!
And I, who dreamed of castles high,
Have only laid the cornerstone.

S/SGT. JARVIS D. ANDERSON

GRANDPARENTS ARE GREAT

All things come to him who waits—provided he knows what he is waiting for.

WOODROW WILSON

The most successful person is the one who holds onto the old just as long as it is good and grabs the new just as soon as it is better.

ROBERT P. VANDERPOOL

Great ideals and principles do not live from generation to generation just because they are right, not even because they have been carefully legislated.

Ideals and principles continue from generation to generation only when they are built into the hearts of the children as they grow up.

GEORGE S. BENSON

The Chinese word for "tomorrow" is composed of two words, "bright day. "

Get over the idea that only children should spend their time in study. Be a student so long as you still have something to learn, and this will mean all your life.

HENRY L. DOHERTY

GRANDPARENTS ARE GREAT

There are many people who are always anticipating trouble, and in this way they manage to enjoy many sorrows that never really happen to them.

JOSH BILLINGS

Look not sorrowfully into the past; it comes not back again. Wisely improve the present; it is thine. Go forth to meet the shadowy future without fear, and with strong heart.

HENRY WADSWORTH LONGFELLOW

An editor about to be beheaded during the French Revolution said:

"It's too bad to take off my head. I wanted to see how this thing was coming out."

SOURCE UNKNOWN

The future fairly startles me with its impending greatness. We are on the verge of undreamed progress.

HENRY FORD

Between the ages of 70 and 83 Commodore Cornelius Vanderbilt added about 100 million dollars to his fortune.

Our grand business in life is not to see what lies dimly at a distance, but to do what lies clearly at hand.

THOMAS CARLYLE

Johann von Goethe at 80 completed *Faust.*
Alfred, Lord Tennyson at 83 wrote "Crossing the Bar."
Titian at 98 painted his famous rendering of the Battle of Lepanto.

GRANDPARENTS ARE GREAT

A little less care for bands of gold,
A little more zest in the days of old;
A broader view and a saner mind,
And a little more love for all mankind;
And so we are faring adown the way
That leads to the gates of a better day.

R. G. WELLS

Our eyes are placed in front because it is more important to look ahead than look back.

. . . Your sons and your daughters shall prophesy, your old men shall dream dreams, your young men shall see visions.

JOEL 2:28b, ACTS 2:17b (KJV)

GRANDPARENTS ARE GREAT

Grow old along with me!
The best is yet to be,
The last of life, for which the first was made.
Our times are in His hand.

ROBERT BROWNING

X

Make it a rule never to regret and never to look back.
Regret is an appalling waste of time.

KATHERINE MANSFIELD

Grandparents Are Great

I am fully aware
That my youth has been spent,
That my get up and go
Has got up and went.

But I really don't mind,
When I think with a grin,
Of all the grand places
My get up has been.

ANONYMOUS

Beauty will mold each thought that lives with me—I shall remember only lovely things.

WILLA HOEY

A young man came for an interview with a bank president.

The young man asked, "Tell me, sir, how did you become so successful?"

The bank president replied, "Two words."

"And what are they, sir?"

"Right decisions."

"How do you make right decisions?"

"One word—experience."

"And how do you get experience?"

"Two words."

"And what are they?"

"Wrong decisions."

SOURCE UNKNOWN

GRANDPARENTS ARE GREAT

It's better to look where you're going than to see where you've been.

In sorrow we learn this truth—we may return to the place of our birth, but we cannot go back to our youth.

JOHN BURROUGHS

GRANDPARENTS ARE GREAT

I learn, as the years roll onward
And I leave the past behind,
That much I had counted sorrow
But proves that God is kind;
That many a flower I had longed for
Had hidden a thorn of pain,
And many a rugged by-path
Led to fields of ripened grain.

KNIGHT'S TREASURY OF ILLUSTRATIONS

GRANDPARENTS ARE GREAT

An old-timer is one who remembers when we could buy a pound of steak for a dime, but forgets we had to work an hour to earn the dime.

We can not control the evil tongues of others, but a good life enables us to despise them.

CATO

GRANDPARENTS ARE GREAT

Some of us can remember when it cost more to run a car than to park it.

I don't think I'd like living in one of those retirement villages. It's easier to tell stories about the "good old days" to people who are too young to contradict me.

ED FRANTZ

Remember when twenty years ago used to be a lot longer ago than it is now?

SOURCE UNKNOWN

GRANDPARENTS ARE GREAT

Lives of great men all remind us
We can make our lives sublime,
And, departing, leave behind us
Footprints on the sand of time—

Footprints, that perhaps another,
Sailing o'er life's solemn main,
A forlorn and shipwrecked brother,
Seeing, shall take heart again.

HENRY WADSWORTH LONGFELLOW

Only one accomplishment is beyond both the power and the mercy of God—
God cannot make the past as though it had never been.

AESCHYLUS

Say not thou, What is the cause that the former days were better than these? for
thou dost not enquire wisely concerning this.

ECCLESIASTES 7:10 (KJV)

Some of us, no matter how difficult the struggles may be, will have to burn some bridges that reach back in memory to an unhappy experience, event, or relationship before we can have any possibility of peace of mind or happiness.

THE MINISTER'S MANUAL FOR 1982

GRANDPARENTS ARE GREAT

Of all sad words
of tongue or pen
The saddest are these:
It might have been.

Let's add this thought
Unto this verse:
It might have been
A great deal worse.

ANONYMOUS

XI

The passing years steal from us
one thing after another.

HORACE

There was the person who was a bit hard of hearing. One day a friend, seeing a loop of wire hanging over the ear, asked, "Do you have a hearing aid?"

"No," came the answer.

"Then why the wire loop over your ear?"

"It causes people to speak louder."

"Could there be anything worse than having a toothache and an earache at the same time?" someone asked Mark Twain.

He replied, "Yes—rheumatism and St. Vitus' Dance, at the same time."

SOURCE UNKNOWN

GRANDPARENTS ARE GREAT

For every ailment under the sun,
There is a remedy, or there is none;
If there be one, try to find it.
If there be none, never mind it.

SOURCE UNKNOWN

GRANDPARENTS ARE GREAT

Why does God send suffering? . . . I heard of a man who was formerly an officer in a church, but who now never goes to church because God took away his daughter . . . . What had God done to that man? Precisely what the man himself had been doing to his own daughter! For the man had sent his daughter to school; . . . he had subjected her to the discipline of learning and to the risk of failure and disappointment; . . . he had encouraged her to play games involving elements of danger. He had set her in an environment that would serve her growth.

GEORGE BUTTRICK

GRANDPARENTS ARE GREAT

Sweet are the uses of adversity;
which, like the toad, ugly and venomous,
wears yet a precious jewel in his head;
and this our life, exempt from public haunt,
Finds tongues in trees, books in the running brooks,
Sermons in stones, and good in every thing.

WILLIAM SHAKESPEARE

I have been reflecting on the inestimable value of "broken things:"

Broken pitchers give ample light for victory—Judges 7:19–21;

Broken bread was more than enough for all the hungry—Matthew 14:19–21

Broken box gave fragrance to all the world—Mark 14:3, 9

Broken body is salvation to all who believe and receive the Saviour—
Isaiah 53:5,6, 12; 1 Corinthians 11:24

and what cannot the Broken One do with our broken plans, projects, dreams, and hearts?

V. RAYMOND EDMAN

GRANDPARENTS ARE GREAT

We are so fond of one another, because our ailments are the same.

JONATHAN SWIFT

The world is full of troubles; it is also full of the overcoming of troubles.

HELEN KELLER

Sidney Smith said in a letter to one of his friends that he is suffering from rheumatism, gout, asthma, and seven other separate complaints. "But apart from that," he said, "I never felt better in my life."

GEORGE H. BOYD

Once John Wesley was walking with a friend whose troubles were vexing him sorely. He told them all to Wesley, and said sadly, "I can't understand it all. If God is love, why have these things come upon me? It is all too much for me. I can't see through it all."

They were walking in the country, and Wesley noticed a cow looking over a wall. He pointed to it and said: "Why does a cow look over a wall?" His friend was surprised, and with a smile he gave the time-honored answer: "Because it can't see through it."

"Precisely," said Wesley, "and if you can't see through your troubles, try looking over them!"

STUART ROBERTSON

GRANDPARENTS ARE GREAT

Everyone knows someone who through God's grace has mastered a grievous physical handicap, risen above some bitter disappointment, won strength from some sorrow, or wrought music out of life's discords.

When caught in some dark night of trouble, it helps to remember someone has been there ahead of us and has won the victory. Such a memory builds confidence and courage. It is a resource for great living.

EVERETT W. PALMER

Grief is a form of unhappiness that comforts.

Grandparents are Great

A mature woman was waiting for a bus. She was very large and crippled with rheumatism. Her arms were loaded with packages.

As the bus door opened, a man waiting behind her offered a helping hand. The woman smiled and shook her head. "I'd best manage alone," she said. "If I get help today—I'll want it tomorrow."

ANONYMOUS

Therefore, my beloved brethren, be ye stedfast, unmoveable, always abounding in the work of the Lord, forasmuch as ye know that your labour is not in vain in the Lord.

1 CORINTHIANS 15:58 (KJV)

An old cowboy said he had learned life's most important lesson from Hereford cows. All his life he had worked cattle ranches where winter storms took a heavy toll among the herds. Freezing rains whipped across the prairies. Howling, bitter winds piled snow into enormous drifts. Temperatures might drop quickly to below zero degrees. Flying ice cut into the flesh. In this maelstrom of nature's violence most cattle would turn the backs to the ice blasts and slowly drift downwind, mile upon mile. Finally, intercepted by a boundary fence, they would pile up against the barrier and die by the scores.

But the Herefords acted differently. Cattle of this breed would instinctively head into the windward end of the range. There they would stand shoulder-to-shoulder facing the storm's blast, heads down against its onslaught. "You always found the Herefords alive and well," said the cowboy. "I guess it's the greatest lesson I ever learned on the prairies—just face life's storms."

GARY BARTON
DEWEY HILLER
JOHN MORANO

XII

Keep your face to the sunshine
and you cannot see the shadow!

HELEN KELLER

GRANDPARENTS ARE GREAT

I walked a mile with Pleasure;
She chatted all the way,
But left me none the wiser
For all she had to say.

I walked a mile with Sorrow,
and ne'er a word said she;
But, oh, the things I learned from her
When Sorrow walked with me!

ROBERT BROWNING HAMILTON

GRANDPARENTS ARE GREAT

There is no greater sorrow than to recall, in misery, the time when we were happy.
DANTE

If one cannot sing as he or she carries their cross, then it would be better to drop it.
ANONYMOUS

GRANDPARENTS ARE GREAT

Sorrows come to stretch out spaces in the heart for joy.

EDWIN MARKHAM

"Who taught thee to sing?" one character asks another in a play by Ibsen.
The answer is: "God sent me a sorrow."

GRANDPARENTS ARE GREAT

Sir Harry Lander lost a son in the first World War. One evening, we are told, he was walking down the street with a small lad at his side. They passed a home where a service flag, bearing a gold star, hung in the window. The boy inquired what that meant. Sir Harry told him that the parents in that home had lost a son at the front.

They walked on for some time in silence and finally they saw the evening star just appearing on the distant horizon. "Look," the boy said, "God is hanging out his service flag. The star is gold. He, too, must a lost a son at the front."

Perhaps that is why God so intimately shares your grief and mine.

FRANCIS W. TRIMMER

Grandparents are Great

I'm cheerful. I'm not always happy, but I'm cheerful. There's a big difference, you know. A happy woman has no cares at all. A cheerful woman has cares and learns to ignore them.

BEVERLY SILLS

What's gone, and what's past help, should be part grief.

WILLIAM SHAKESPEARE

What . . . can we say at times of tragedy?

I. We can say that God is as grieved as we are, that he is sharing in our sorrow and grief, that he is afflicted in all our afflictions, that his heart is going out to meet our hearts.

II. We can say that . . . there is a life to come, and in that life God is seeing to it that life cut off too soon is getting its chance to blossom and flourish . . . .

III. We can say that Christianity has never pretended to explain sorrow and suffering . . . . In any disaster the reason may well lie in human error.

IV. We can say that what Christianity does triumphantly offer is the power to face tragedy, to bear it, to come through on our own two feet, and even to transform it so that the tragedy becomes a crown.

WILLIAM BARCLAY

Some weeks ago, my brother who is a minister in Memphis sent me a copy of one of his sermons. In it was the story of a young man whose wife had died, leaving him with a small son.

Back home from the cemetery on the day of the funeral, they went to bed early because in his sorrow the young widower could think of nothing else he could bear to do. As he lay there in the darkness, grief-stricken, numb with sorrow, the little boy broke the stillness from his little bed with a disturbing question: "Daddy, where is Mommy?"

The young father tried to get the boy to go to sleep, but the questions kept coming from his confused childish mind: "Where is Mommy?" "When is she coming home?"

After a while, the father got up and brought the little boy to bed with him. But the child was still disturbed and restless . . . and persistent with his probing, heartbreaking questions.

Finally, the little boy reached out his hand through the darkness and placed it on his father's face asking: "Daddy, is your face toward me?"

Given assurance, both verbally and by his own touch that his father's face was indeed toward him, the little boy said: "If your face is toward me, I think I can go to sleep." And in a little while he was quiet.

The father lay there in the darkness and in childlike faith, he lifted up his own needy heart to his Father in heaven and prayed: "O God, the way is dark and I confess that I do not see my way through right now, but if your face is toward me, somehow I think I can make it."

JAMES MOORE

XIII

To live in hearts we leave behind—
Is not to die.

THOMAS CAMPBELL

GRANDPARENTS ARE GREAT

Baron von Hugel said, "I will wait for the breath of God. Perhaps he will call me today, tonight. I would like to finish my book, but if not, I shall live it out in the beyond."

M. H. LICHLITER

Excuse of grief for the dead is madness; for it is an injury to the living, and the dead know it not.

XENOPHON

GRANDPARENTS ARE GREAT

Little Ruth had died when she was only three years old.

Many years later her mother said, "When I get to heaven, I will not care whether the gates are pearl or wood; I will not care if the streets are paved with gold or with concrete. I want to see Ruth—that will be heaven for me."

GRANDPARENTS ARE GREAT

In his hand is the life of every creature and the breath of all mankind.

BENJAMIN FRANKLIN

May your deeds be shown to your servants, your splendor to their children.

PSALM 90:16 (NIV)

GRANDPARENTS ARE GREAT

Let those who thoughtfully consider the brevity of life remember the length of eternity.

BISHOP THOMAS KEN

Practically all the progress that man has made is due to the fact that he is mortal. If man knew that his days on earth were to be endless, all incentive to better himself—except to seek food and clothing—would be lost. There would be no desire to make his mark in the world; no stimulating ambition to leave the world a little better than he found it; no hungry aspiration to be remembered after he is dead. If there were no death, life would become a thing stagnant, monotonous, and unspeakably burdensome.

ROBERT W. MACKENNA

In my Father's house are many rooms; if it were not so, I would have told you. I am going there to prepare a place for you. And if I go and prepare a place for you, I will come back and take you to be with me that you also may be where I am.

JOHN 14:2, 3 (NIV)

"And this is the will of him who sent me, that I shall lose none of all that he has given me, but raise them up at the last day. For my Father's will is that everyone who looks to the Son and believes in him shall have eternal life, and I will raise him up at the last day."

JOHN 6:39, 40 (NIV)

GRANDPARENTS ARE GREAT

The time must come when I shall sleep
A slumber long, and soft and deep.
I shall not hear, I shall not see
Nor suffer this mortality.

This sleep is not to be the end
But stripped of flesh my soul will spend
Eternity in calm and peace
And know the fulness of release.

GRANDPARENTS ARE GREAT

Where it is I do not know,
This final place to which I go.
It may be near, it may be far,
It could exist upon a star.

But this existence I am sure
Through the ages will endure
And though my frame lies under sod
My Soul forever lives with God.

JOHN TOWNSEND

XIV

O God, thou hast taught me from my youth:
and hitherto have I declared thy wondrous works.

Now also when I am old and grey-headed,
O God, forsake me not;
until I have shewed thy strength unto this generation . . . .
PSALM 71:17, 18 (KJV)

Martin Luther sometimes succumbed to depression. During a time when he was passing through a "fiery trial," his wife Cathy, dressed in black, entered his study. She said, "God is dead!"

"Nonsense, woman, God lives!" answered Luther.

"Then," she replied, "if you believe that God is living, act like it. Live like it!"

SOURCE UNKNOWN

More things are wrought by prayer than this world dreams of.

Alfred, Lord Tennyson

To be distracted—look within;
To be defeated—look back;
To be distracted—look around;
To be dismayed—look before;
To be delivered—look to Christ;
To be delighted—look up.

Anonymous

GRANDPARENTS ARE GREAT

Thou art coming to a King,
Large petitions with thee bring
For His grace and power are such
None can ever ask too much.

JOHN NEWTON

An atheist is one who has no invisible means of support.

Trust says, "I may not know what the future holds, but I know Who holds the future."

This is what I found out about religion: It gives you courage to make the decisions you must make in a crisis and the confidence to leave the results to a higher Power.

DWIGHT D. EISENHOWER

What Jesus Does for Me:

He gives me grace and strength to try, at least, things that I know are impossible, and to attempt, first of all, the things that are hardest to be done.

He helps me refuse to do good when I know that something better can be done.

He helps me to keep on when I have to, even though I know I cannot.

ROBERT E. SPEER

Bishop McDowell put it this way: "We are saved by a Person and only a Person, and, as far as I know, by only one Person."

SOURCE UNKNOWN

The LORD bless thee, and keep thee: The LORD make his face shine upon thee, and be gracious unto thee: The LORD lift up his countenance upon thee, and give thee peace.

NUMBERS 6:24-26 (KJV)